A PRACTICAL GUIDE: BLACK HAIR CARE

TERRIA ROUSHUN EPTING

Table of Contents

INTRODUCTION

*T*his guide was written to help you, the transracial adoptive or foster parent of Black children, help your child thrive through the love of their hair.

This means that as the parent, you must learn to love their hair too. To do that, you must first be equipped with the knowledge, skillset, and confidence required.

I understand that afro-textured, kinky, curly, tightly coiled hair can be a challenge to those who have never worked with this varied hair fabric.

Save heart! This guide was written specifically for you with compassion, informed care, and a lot of encouragement.

You can do this! Let's begin.

HOW TO USE THIS GUIDE

This guide is no different from others, flowing sequentially to ensure the reader arrives at a desired end. You might be tempted to skip a section or even skim through each section, but I encourage you to be patient and stay the course.

Until now, most of your focus may have been on products and styling techniques. The internet is certainly bombarded with messages centered around the "right" products. While products and styling are important there is something more important than either of those.

Let's start there.

BLACK HAIR & THE TRANSRACIAL ADOPTIVE/FOSTER FAMILY

*H*aving trained hundreds of transracial adoptive or foster parents of Black children, I've noticed that the main challenges are feelings of overwhelmedness, anxiety, and stress as these parents embark on this hair journey. Even parents who have been on this hair journey for several years say the same.

I discovered, in most cases, at the root of this anxiety is a lack of *belief* that they can be successful. Many parents don't recognize that they come into parenthood of a Black child with some underlying preconceptions about kinky hair and Black culture overall. Here is a story that was shared with me:

Jenn is a wife and mom of two: a biological 8-year-old daughter and a 4-year-old African American daughter. With her cousin's wedding looming at the end of the week she knew she had to remove the braids from her daughter's hair (which had been in too long), shampoo, and style it for the wedding. With each passing day she would tell herself, "Tomorrow is hair day". And with each day she felt more anxious and stressed about the task. The week progressed, life happened, but hair time didn't! The morning of the wedding Jenn was incredibly wound up as she attempted to do her daughter's kinky hair. The child had a meltdown, Jenn had a meltdown, and time slipped away. In the end, Jenn's husband and son went to the wedding without them.

Here we have a missed life event because Jenn wasn't equipped to do her daughter's hair. What's more, she had experienced four years of stress, meltdowns, and anxiety at hair time. It doesn't have to be this way!

Jenn and I began to work together to find out what is at the root of her anxiety about her child's hair. Additionally, we explored her current knowledge, skillset, and emotions. Jenn was a bit surprised at what lay at the root of her angst. We used the assessment on the next page to guide our discovery and I encourage you to do the same.

Assessment is the first step.

SELF ASSESSMENT

*T*he purpose of this assessment is to reveal your past and current experiences, product knowledge, and feelings or thoughts as it relates to managing your child's kinky, curly, tightly coiled hair. Remember, no judgment. Just be honest with yourself! Acknowledgment of your starting place will lead to much success down the road!

Answer True or False to the following:

PRODUCT KNOWLEDGE

_____ I have experimented with different products and have narrowed down what works for me

_____ I know the best products to use for my child's hair type

_____ I have no idea what products to use for my child's hair type

_____I frequently buy products from the ethnic hair care aisle

__ _I am often frustrated and confused when shopping in the ethnic aisle

_____I don't shop in the ethnic hair care aisle

_____I am aware of products designed to release the curl for easier comb through

_____I typically use the same products on my child's hair that I use on my own

_____I have spent money on products that didn't work for us

__ _I rely on pictures and in-store merchandising to make a purchase decision

_____ I determine my product selections based on what I see and hear on social media

TEXTURED HAIR KNOWLEDGE True/False

__I can identify the different types of textured hair

__I can Identify my child's hair type and texture

__Textured hair is structurally different from straight hair

__I have watched videos on YouTube, FB, Instagram, ALL OF THE THINGS in search of help with my child's hair and I still don't know the essentials for good hair care

__ I usually seek out other people to ask for help

EMOTIONAL True/False

__I tend to feel anxious when it's time to care for my child's hair

__I will let my child's hair go "undone" vs dealing with it

__I have self-doubt about learning how to manage kinky hair

__I believe this hair is difficult to work with

__I have joined online groups that are helpful

__I have joined online groups that are not helpful

__I have been looking for support and I am open to it

EXPERIENCE True/False

__I have experience with textured hair other than my child's

__I have developed a successful strategy for caring for textured hair, it works for me

__I usually feel good about the outcome of the style I created

__I have a difficult time working with textured hair, it's overwhelming!

__ I am willing to invest time to learn and practice

__I do not know how to properly detangle my child's hair

__I am better than I used to be in managing my child's hair but still need help

__I am confident in my ability and can teach others!

__I am open to learning new things

DIG DEEPER

This part of the assessment is still non-judgmental. It is just the facts. You don't have to write anything down. Remember to be honest within yourself and grant yourself some grace!

Take time and think of these before you answer:

1. I have always seen the beauty of black hair (True/False)

2. Think about when you first became aware of Black hair. Can you remember how old you were? (Assess your thoughts, feelings, or questions you had about it.)

3. What were you told/taught about Black hair as a child (overtly or covertly)?

4. What was your early exposure to kinky, curly, coily hair? Did you grow up with a Black friend with kinky, curly, coily hair? College friend?

5. Have you used negative words to describe your Black child's hair? What were they?

How did that assessment feel? What did you uncover about your deeper thoughts, feelings, or ideas about kinky, curly, tightly coiled hair? Do you feel equipped to care for your child's hair? How confident are you that you can learn how to give good care to your child's kinky hair?

Now is a good time to take a deep breath! You can release all of that anxiety. You're on the right track. After all, It's only hair... actually, it's more than hair.

Let's explore a bit of history.

9

A BIT OF BLACK HAIR HISTORY

The beauty standard in this country, and worldwide, has always focused on long, lush, flowing hair. Afro-textured hair does not grow long or straight. It tends to grow up and out. Therefore, beauty standards have always excluded afro-textured hair.

Not long ago, Eurocentric beauty was and, in some industries, remains the beauty standard. Images of lusciously long, flowing hair were the only images you saw on television, magazines, runways, cartoons, toys and product packaging.

However, it wasn't always like that. In Africa, hair was celebrated! It was described as a crown. Marital status, social status, and beauty were portrayed by the thick, tightly coiled hair that was often intricately braided or woven with various materials. Yes, a crown indeed!

During slavery, everything changed. Tightly coiled hair, being so unique and different, was described as animal hair, wooly, unruly, and unkempt. Hair became another way to dehumanize Black people.

The years after emancipation, Black men and women would straighten their hair to conform and be accepted. In fact, the first Black millionaire, Madam C. J. Walker, made her millions with haircare products that promised to keep afro-textured, kinky, tightly coiled hair straight.

The stigmatization of Black hair still exists to this day. In a recent study, children as young as kindergarten age report being discriminated against because of their hair. We know children are sent home and even expelled from school for wearing their natural hair and hairstyles. In another study, 100 teen girls were interviewed and 80% experienced discrimination because of their hair and bodies.

We know this carries into the workplace. I personally experienced this discrimination when a supervisor told me during a raving performance review I would "probably get promoted if I would do something different with my hair"!

Recently, legislation was enacted to stop such discrimination! In 2019, State Senator Holly Mitchell introduced the Crown Act. It passed that same year in California and was signed into California law. The Crown Act demands protection against race-based hair discrimination based on hair texture and protective hairstyles in the workplace and K-12 in public and charter schools.

In March of 2022, the House of Representatives passed the H. R. 2116 Bill, Create a Respectful and Open World for Natural Hair, C.R.O.W.N. act. It now awaits the Senate to pass into law. Meanwhile, only 18 States have adopted this as State law. As of this writing, the C.R.O.W.N. Act, H R 2116 Bill, failed to pass the Senate.

There is much work yet to be done to end discrimination against afro-textured hair. So, the next time you wonder, or someone asks, "What's the big deal about afro-textured hair anyway?" You have a bit of history you can ponder or share.

One of the best ways you can equip your child and build their confidence is to learn how to care for their hair.

WHY YOU SHOULD PROVIDE CARE FOR YOUR BLACK CHILD'S HAIR

*I*n most major cities and the surrounding areas, there are hair salons and barber shops that cater to afro-textured hair. As an adoptive or foster parent of a Black child, you might think it's easier or it's best to take your child to someone else for hair care and grooming.

Nothing could be farther from the truth! Given the statistics and the history of afro-textured hair, it is imperative that you, as the parent, affirm your child and equip them to maneuver the discrimination they will inevitably face. And, most of all, to teach them to love their hair and affirm their beauty.

Time spent patiently learning how to properly care for your child's hair can be a bonding experience that matures over the years. Growing up as one of five children, I can remember hair time was the only time I had my mom, and occasionally my dad, to myself. Culturally, hair time with a parent, sibling, older family member, and even peers can mean *I love you, I care about you*, and *you are important to me*!

Another reason that you should provide the care for your child's hair is that the journey into afro-textured hair can be a journey into Black culture. You learn styles, lingo, history, what's considered beautiful, what's on trend, etc. I have encountered many adult transracial adoptees who continue to experience shame and sometimes anger because they were not taught cultural nuances and especially those that pertain to their hair!

Let's take a look at the structural differences of afro-textured hair when compared to the hair of other ethnicities.

WHY IS AFRO-TEXTURED HAIR SO DIFFERENT?

Hair Structure

*T*ypically, everyone has hair. The type of hair we have on our heads is determined by ethnicity. When comparing the cellular structural shape of Caucasian hair, it tends to be round or oval shaped while that of African descent is curved in shape with flat hair follicles. This causes the hair to grow tightly coiled. Additionally, this causes the hair to have a different texture than round-celled hair. Most other ethnicities resemble the structural shape of Caucasian which is why afro-textured hair seems so unique and different.

Other than that, the basic structure of hair is the same. Each strand has a hair shaft and a hair follicle (root).

There's one other thing that may help clarify the dryness that is typical for afro-textured hair. We all produce something called sebum, as the hair follicle is connected to the sebaceous gland. Sebum is a natural oil/lubricant. With Caucasian round-cell hair (which grows straighter), it is easier for the oil to travel down the strands as a natural lubricant (sometimes a bit too oily). With afro-textured hair, the sebum must move through zigs and zags, kinks and coils! Needless to say, it doesn't make it all the way down the hair shaft thus making the texture of afro hair drier in appearance and feel.

That's it. Mystery solved!

Hair Type vs Texture

Hair typing as we know it today is relatively new. You may have seen hair charts that give hair a type of grade from 1A to 4C, with 1A being the straightest hair type and 4C being the tightest coiled. Initially it was used as a marketing guide. Yes, marketers realized that in order to sell more products they can "typecast" hair so that we, the consumers, would know which of their products is best for our hair.

As the natural hair community grew and Black people were embracing their natural hair more and more, community members jumped on the hair type bandwagon and still consider this as a useful guide to determine what's best for their hair. You can decide if this is useful or not. Most transracial adoptive and foster parents of Black children find this chart quite confusing. I agree. Instead, I like to teach parents to focus on the hair their child has. It doesn't really matter the type it is.

The one thing you should be aware of is your child will typically have more than one texture of hair on their head. It's best to learn what is the most dominant hair texture and work with that.

Hair texture mostly refers to the thickness of the strands and the number of strands on the head. Consider this illustration:

> There is a grove of trees with a significant number of thin, reed-like trees in it. There are so many of

these thin trees that you cannot see from one end of the grove to the next. It's very dense. This can describe thin or fine hair with a thick texture.

Conversely, there is a grove with large oak trees. The trees are large but if you maneuver around you can see across the grove because of the spaces between them. This would describe thick hair with thin texture.

The third grove has medium sized trees that are densely packed together making it hard to see from one end of the grove to the next. This would describe thick hair with thick texture.

This is important to know because it will dictate the types of products that will work best, the number of products you should use, and even the styles that will work best on your child's hair.

We'll get to style later but first we should consider one of the most important characteristics of your child's hair, porosity level.

HAIR POROSITY TEST

Take a clean strand of a hair and place it into transparent glass of water, Leave & wait for 3 minutes.

Low Hair Porosity	Normal Hair Porosity	High Hair Porosity

Absorbs & do not releases the moisture easily	Absorbs & retain the moisture moderately	Absorbs & releases the moisture easily

Porosity

Hair porosity is defined as a measurement of the hair's ability to absorb and hold moisture, how fast moisture penetrates the hair, and how long it stays. Porosity is usually determined by genetics although external factors can impact the hair's ability to absorb moisture. Professionally, I believe this measurement is more important than knowing hair type.

We discussed earlier that afro-textured hair tends to be dry due to the lack of natural oil distributed throughout the strands. Therefore, we must use products to ensure the hair is receiving the moisture it needs to thrive. A bit more about this when we discuss products.

Porosity is measured by Low, Medium, and High:

Low Porosity – The cuticles on the hair shaft (the strand) are tightly packed together and lay flat. While this can indicate healthy hair, it also makes it difficult for nutrients and moisture to penetrate. Low porosity hair requires patience to work the product into the hair until it is absorbed. If the product is not absorbed, low

21

porosity hair can easily become dry and brittle which leads to breakage. Once the product is absorbed, it doesn't easily dissipate.

Medium Porosity – While this seems to be the preferred porosity level, it is important to maintain the levels of moisture for optimal results. This can be achieved by identifying the moisture cycle (see Moisture Cycle). Additionally, medium porosity hair can be easily affected by external factors like weather, chemical applications, heat styling, etc.

High Porosity – The cuticles on high porosity hair are lifted on the shaft. This is usually caused by some sort of external damage and the culprit is usually excessive heat styling and chemical treatments although it can be genetically informed as well. With larger gaps on the cuticles, the product is absorbed rapidly. Unfortunately, the moisture tends to dissipate equally as rapidly. High porosity hair almost always needs to have the moisture sealed in with oil.

Porosity Tests

There are several methods you can use to test the porosity of your child's hair. With each of these methods, your child's hair must be freshly clean and dry to get an accurate test:

Method 1: Float Test – In a clear glass with room temperature water place a strand of your child's hair in it. Does the hair sink immediately or relatively quickly? That suggests *High Porosity*. Does it hang out on the top of the water or just beneath the surface? That suggests *Low Porosity*. Hair that sinks midway relatively easily, that's *Medium Porosity*.

Method 2: Spray Test – On freshly shampooed, unconditioned, and air-dried hair, mist the hair with a spray bottle of water (no need to saturate). Does the water tend to bead up and sit on the top of the hair? That suggests *Low Porosity*. Does the water disappear quickly? That suggests *High porosity*. Note: This method is best done on a small section of hair in two places: one near the front/top of the head and one near the back/nape. Also, it is the most cumbersome test since you must have clean, unconditioned, and air dried hair (without heat).

As you can see, knowing the porosity levels can guide you to the right products for your child's hair. It also will dictate the frequency of hair time you should incorporate and will help identify the moisture cycle.

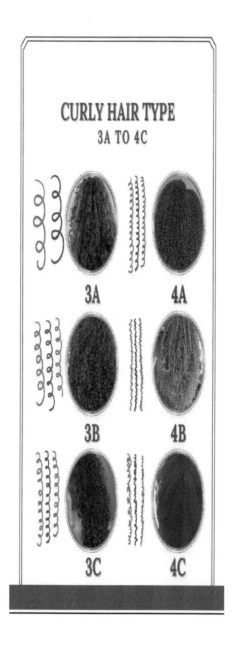

<u>Moisture Cycle</u>

The moisture cycle refers to how often you need to add moisture to your child's hair. It can vary from person to person, season to season. To identify your child's hair moisture cycle:

1. Make sure you know – or have an idea of – the porosity level

2. Assess how soon after a fresh shampoo, conditioning treatment, and styling the hair *feels* dry to the touch. Don't go by the way it looks, this is a touch-and-feel exercise

3. If it feels different, drier, or rougher than it did when it was first shampooed and styled, this is an indicator to add moisture

4. Make note of how many days passed before you needed to add moisture again. **This is your child's hair moisture cycle.**

5. Don't be alarmed if you find your child's hair requires moisture added daily

6. Be sparing with the product you choose to avoid product build-up

7. Sleeping in a silky bonnet, scarf, or durag will keep the cotton pillowcases and sheets from robbing the hair of moisture

Surface Texture

You may recall I mentioned the importance of determining the moisture cycle by how the hair feels vs how it looks. Hair has what is called "surface texture." Becoming familiar with your child's surface texture can help you understand why it may appear dry after you have done the steps to moisturize and hydrate the hair.

Here's a demonstration exercise. Consider two leather handbags. One is black cowhide leather and the other is patent leather. If I were to wipe them both down with a leather cleaner/conditioner product and then make sure both are completely dry I can then assess the surface of each after cleaning.

Clearly, the patent leather is shiner on the surface than the other. They are both leather, they are both clean, and they are both dry. However, one has a naturally shiny appearance and the other is matte and duller. Does it mean the matte one is any less clean? Or any less conditioned from the leather cleaner? No! The natural surface of the patent leather is shiny and more reflective of light than the plain cowhide one. There is no need to add more leather conditioner to the matte one simply because it looks dull!

It's the same with hair surface texture. Just because it appears dry and dull does not mean it is! Adding more and more product only leads to build-up.

Determining a moisture cycle is one of those areas where you will need to trust your instincts, Moms and Dads! As you continue the hair journey with your child, you will be able to identify the surface texture and learn exactly what your child's hair needs to thrive. You can do it!

Let's discuss the essentials.

3 ESSENTIALS AREAS OF BLACK HAIR CARE

*C*ontrary to what social media might say, there are only three essential areas that you as the parent of a Black child need to focus on when it comes to caring for their hair. These areas are shampoo/conditioning, detangling, and styling.

Shampoo

There are many theories about how often to shampoo and avoid drying out the hair. The rule of thumb is every seven to 10 days. As with other rules, this is made to be broken too!

When considering how often to shampoo your child's hair given their age:

The 7–10 day rule should not apply to your infant or toddler! The follicles on infant hair are immature and will change through ages two or three.

An infant typically needs a daily soft rinsing at bath time, a weekly gentle shampoo with minimal products (maybe a lite oil), and gentle brushing with the softest baby brush. The brushing will stimulate the scalp and keep conditions like cradle cap at bay.

A toddler may need more frequent shampooing than every 7-10 days because they are on the move! They put things in and on their hair. Sand at the beach, dirt at the playground, and even mashed potatoes at dinner! Your toddler's shampoo routine will depend on their activity and will probably change from week to week. Try not to go longer than the 7-10 days before shampooing, however.

Your older children may need to shampoo once per week at a minimum depending on their activity, like sports. Boys with typically shorter hair can shampoo even more frequently. If their hair is kept short or cropped to their scalp with frequent cuts, they continually have new growth and no need to worry about overdoing it with shampoo.

WHICH SHAMPOO TO CHOOSE?

*T*here is probably more shampoo on the store shelves than in any other product category. Each one promises the holy grail of shiny, moist, and soft hair! The goal of shampoo for your Black child's hair should be one thing: to cleanse the hair without stripping the hair of its natural oils.

If you recall, we discussed sebum, the natural oil we all produce that is typically in short supply on kinky, curly coily hair. Your choice of shampoo should be void of the most common culprits that rob afro-textured hair of their natural oils. The most typical are parabens, sulfur, silicones, paraffins, and mineral oils. Here is a general guide when selecting a shampoo:

<u>Moisturizing shampoos</u> are well received by all textures and porosity levels of afro-textured hair. There are many brands to choose from at various price points.

Clarifying shampoos should be used sparingly. Sometimes hair, particularly thick hair, with a lot of product use causing build-up will require an occasional clarifying shampoo. These shampoos are very drying on afro-textured hair. It's best to do one clarifying shampoo followed by a moisturizing shampoo and an appropriate rinse-out conditioner.

Treatment shampoos like those with added protein should only be used if the hair is showing signs of stress and weakness like excessive shedding or breaking. However, with too much use, protein shampoos and treatments can coat the hair and make it more difficult for moisture to penetrate thus causing further damage.

While we are speaking of cleansing the hair, I want to dispel a huge myth: Water does not dry out your child's hair! Water is the most moisturizing substance you can apply to your child's hair so use it often.

CONDITIONING

Shampooing and conditioning go hand in hand. Always. Remember, the sebum we discussed earlier? Well, with every shampoo a bit of the hair's natural oil is lost. Conditioners serve to replace some of the moisture and hydration lost during shampooing. It also serves as a detangling product.

There are several types of conditioners on the market that are designed to address different concerns:

Daily Conditioner – These leave-in products are designed to give that quick blast of moisture to the hair and a bit of "slip" for easy detangling. Identifying your child's Moisture Cycle will help determine your use of a daily conditioner.

Rinse Out Conditioner – Typically used immediately following a shampoo, these are designed to penetrate the hair shaft and add moisture while the cuticles are open during the shampoo.

Deep Conditioner – These are designed to remain on the hair for a specified amount of time following

34

a shampoo before rinsing. They add high levels of moisture to the hair, softening and detangling the hair for easier manageability. Most often are used one to two times per month because of the time factor although it can be used once per week.

Hair Mask – These are different from deep conditioners in that they are designed to address specific issues like extreme dryness, weak strands, or hair shedding. Masks should be used one time per month as needed.

A good rule of thumb when selecting conditioner(s) is to consider the porosity and texture (thickness) of your child's hair. Here is a general guide:

Low Porosity – All types of conditioners can be used. However, the hair shaft is tight and hard to penetrate so if using a thick cream, it must be patiently worked into the hair. Lighter creams or liquid formulations, like a hair milk, might be a better choice for low porosity hair.

High Porosity – Heavy creams and butters are good because the large gaps on the hair shaft make it easy to absorb. These heavy, rich conditioners are especially good on thick textures with high porosity. Keep in mind high porosity hair must be sealed with oil after the cream/butter type of conditioners to seal in the moisture.

A Note on Oil

Oils are not moisturizers. They are sealants. By rubbing hair oil on the strands after cleansing, conditioning, or simply misting with water, the moisture will be sealed in the hair shaft a bit longer. Conversely, if you oil the strands while the hair is dry and thirsty, well, you are sealing in that dryness. It will be difficult for moisture to penetrate the strands after being oiled. Oils can be lightly used to help soothe a dry and itchy scalp if there is no medical issue causing excessive scalp dryness or itch. When in doubt please consult a dermatologist or your pediatrician.

DETANGLING

Detangling afro-textured hair gives moms and dads of all races a challenge when caring for their Black child's hair. Because the hair zigs and zags on kinky, curly, and coily hair, it tends to tangle easily and even become matted and difficult to detangle. Couple that with a squirming child, or one with a tender head or sensory challenges, and you can feel overwhelmed and hopeless.

Following these steps will help alleviate this challenge:

1. Be consistent with the detangling process. It may even be best to detangle daily rather than waiting until shampoo time. That means if your child has braids (plait styles) or twists, you can undo them one at a time each day, add moisture, and detangle to keep the tangles at bay. Also, the consistency will teach your child that sitting for detangling doesn't have to be too dramatic.

2. Use a product with good "slip". This simply means using a slippery conditioner and/or water to make sure your fingers and tools can glide through the hair.

3. Start with your fingers! The tighter the coils the more beneficial using fingers is because you can get up close and personal with the kinks and coils.

4. Using a comb or a detangling brush, gather a section and add a sufficient amount of product, starting at the ends of the hair. Begin to gently comb or brush the tangles out as you move up the section towards the scalp. Have your spray bottle with water handy and add more as needed.

5. Continue this process until all the hair is completely detangled.

6. It's best to detangle in small sections. The longer and thicker the hair, the smaller the sections should be.

NOTE: Always detangle hair completely BEFORE shampooing.

If you are detangling hair prior to shampoo, section hair using your fingers and massage in the product of your choice while separating any tangles. If detangling dry hair and preparing for styling, section hair in the desired style – you may need to add product during this step – (i.e. 4 quadrants, or a part down the middle), and secure each part with a clip. Divide that section as necessary for easier detangling, depending on the thickness and length of the hair then generously apply the product of choice.

Two tools you should have in your detangling arsenal are a detangling brush and comb.

DETANGLE COMB - This is any wide-tooth comb. Be sure to match the right tool to the hair type and length you are detangling. For example, you may be tempted to try to use a very wide-toothed comb on very short hair, but it won't completely catch all the kinks and detangle it.

DETANGLE BRUSH - I typically will grab a detangling brush first, especially when working with short hair. The brush (usually plastic) can glide through the coils and kinks a bit more forgiving than when using a comb.

STYLING

Most moms and dads tell me they are most eager to learn this area because it's the part that is seen by others and this is how they are being judged. Here are some things to consider:

1. You won't become a stylist but you can learn your child's hair so grant yourself grace.

2. Don't focus on the fancy skills you see demonstrated on social media. There are classic everyday styles that are easy to learn and practice.

3. Consider your lifestyle when selecting an everyday style. Do you tend to be in a hurry to get out the door most days? If so, a style that can last a few days to a week, like plaits, may be best.

4. Be open to continuous training to build your skillset.

Deciding on a style that works for your child's hair will take some research. Consider the following:

Infants/Toddlers – less is best. Their hair will change and their scalp is still soft in spots. A simple rinse at bath time and a gentle shampoo occasionally are all that's required. Be sure to gently brush (with a soft baby brush) daily to keep cradle cap at bay. Tight bands, braids, bows, and barrettes are not a necessity at this time. Neither are heavy styling products.

Boys – styling trends for young boys have become more creative recently. The same rules apply to boys as girls when determining a style. Consider their hair texture, best products, and your lifestyle. The easiest style is closely cropped hair. An easy brush through in the morning and they are good to go. A fade on the sides with a bit of hair on top is another easy style. Just add a bit of moisture on the longer part, brush the sides, and you are out the door! Another current style is cropped hair with creative designs cut into it. Braids (cornrows and plaits) are pretty much on trend for boys. Of course, the age of your son should be considered when choosing a style.

Young girls – No matter their length or texture, the styling for younger girls typically involves braids, twists, ponytails, and puffs. These are more contained styles. At a younger age they are active and not as aware of what is going on with their hair so wearing their hair out – like in an afro—is not the best way to keep it healthy and knot-free. A lot of hair accessories are used for this age group.

Junior high – By this time they will be able to communicate the type of styles they are interested in. They begin to want to take the reins and do their own hair more often than not. For sure the styles will become more creative as seen on social media. This is not the time for you, moms and dads, to back completely off. The care of their hair is still important.

You will probably require additional training to learn the right styles for your child and how to execute them. However, Once you got it...you got It!

LIST OF KEY PRODUCTS & TOOLS

Moisture Shampoo – best for all types of afro-textured hair

Leave-In Conditioner – best when daily added moisture is necessary

Rinse out Conditioner – used immediately following shampoo to soften hair for styling

Styling product (cream or gel) – the final step of moisture before sealing with oil

Oil – used to seal in moisture. Applied over hair after conditioners or moisturizing styling products

Spray bottle – to hold the water which is vital during hair time

Wide tooth comb – great for detangling and combing through thick hair

Detangling brush – used on wet or dry hair and is designed to move through tangles

Rattail comb – best used for parting the hair

Clippers – for home trims, linings, and haircuts

Boar bristle/Natural brush – great for smoothing hair as you gather it into a band or tie, helps to blend styling product into hair

Hair Bonnet/Silky pillowcase – to protect hair from rough surfaces like cotton sheets

Silky scarf – used to secure a hairstyle in place

Rubber Bands – holds hair in place in sections. It's best to remove at night by snipping them off with scissors to keep from tangling in hair

Hair ties – Gentler on the hair than rubber bands, come in an assortment of styles and fabrics

VISITING A PROFESSIONAL

The focus of this guide is to support you on how to give care to your child's hair. However, there are times when you should take your child to a Black hair care professional.

Culturally, the Black-owned, Black ran barber shop or beauty shop is not only to provide hair care services, but also a safe place where Black men, women and children come to socialize, discuss current topics, be celebrated and to share values. It's a place of pride since they are owned and operated by Black people. Imagine never having experienced that sense of community as a Black adult. As the parent of a Black child, it is important to visit a Black salon or barber shop with your child for these reasons.

The age and frequency at which this happens depends on you as the parent. You don't want your child to be too young for example, he may be afraid of the buzz of the clippers which can lead to a traumatic experience. Growing up starting around age eight, my beauty shop visits happened twice a year, Easter, and Christmas. Those were special occasions and I looked forward to the lively conversations and laughter. Going to the beauty shop was a rite of passage for my sisters and I!

To be transparent, as a boy mom I did not like taking him to the barbershop, even though I had to at times when my husband was away. I felt like I was intruding in a men's club! The men seemed to be a bit more reserved, not as loud whenever women are present. But I went anyway because I knew as a hair professional myself the importance of it. If there are no Black barber or beauty shops in your area, may I suggest you intentionally, at least a few times per year, seek one out.

Most times, a recommendation for a barber or stylist is best. Keep in mind some professionals work better with children than others.

ENGAGEMENT BUILDS CONFIDENCE

*H*air time can be a time of bonding with your child. Sometimes when I say this to clients, parents correct me and say, "That can never be true in my house! Hair time is a stressful battle!" I always ask how they engage *before, during and after* hair time? Engagement is important because:

- It signals the routine

- It involves the child in the process

- Develops a sense of responsibility (i.e., gathering items)

- It opens communication and builds trust

The haircare routine can start days even weeks before you do it. This can be in the form of selecting hair accessories at the store and looking at styles in magazines together. Discussing your child's hair and how it differs from yours should begin as early as possible. I read once that Black children growing up in predominantly white environments (boys and girls) will notice the difference in their hair before they notice a difference in their skin. Age-appropriate hair talks will prove to be vital to bonding.

Your child can be engaged in hair time at any age. Here are some examples of engagement:

- Be responsible for getting the "hair chair"

- Gather the box of tools, barrettes & accessories

- Practice learning their colors by organizing the color of the day

- Practice counting

Doing any age-appropriate activity together as you prepare for hair time will calm nerves all the way around.

Finding ways to engage in discussions about your child's hair as a part of everyday life, builds not only your child's confidence but yours too. Your child's kinky, curly, and coily hair should not be only addressed when it is time to do the task. These discussions can focus on other cultural subject matters (age appropriate). Always

48

be sure to remain aware of your emotions, anxiety, or stress levels. Your child will pick up on your vibe for sure. If you are confident and at ease about hair time, your child will be too.

FINAL WORDS

I truly believe that anyone reading this can learn to give care to kinky, curly, tightly coiled hair. I also know it requires *believing* you can, up-leveling your skill set, and understanding you are on a journey. A journey that will go deeper than hair and can lead to a family that thrives!

Begin to affirm yourself, trust yourself, and celebrate your small wins.

This journey requires different skills at different ages. It requires different cultural understandings at different stages. It requires strength to stand up and face off against people who may not agree with the makeup of your family. It will require practice, continuous training and it may require a mentor.

One thing for sure? It will require that you give yourself grace.

ABOUT THE AUTHOR

Terria Roushun is the CEO and Owner of the Hair Essentials Company and Director of Love & Coils, a membership group that offers support to parents on a hair journey with their Black child.

Terria has a keen eye for trend looks and her hand-perfecting skill has afforded her the opportunity to work with several prestige brands and agencies in New York, Los Angeles, and in the Chicagoland area. More recently she began to help the transracial adoptive and foster community overcome the anxiety of dealing with highly textured hair. Hair Essentials Company is designed specifically with that community in mind.

From a young age, it was instilled in Terria to use her gifts to serve others. Throughout her formative years, she always kept that notion in the back of her mind, what are my gifts and how can they help others? Today, Terria is celebrated for spreading positivity, empowering families and turning trend looks into everyday fashions.

Terria has expanded her one-on- one private session to include group training in order to share her methods with a larger scope of transracial adoptive and foster parents.

HAIRCARE OPENS THE DOOR TO BONDING

AFFIRMING YOUR CHILDS BEAUTY BUILDS
SELF ESTEEM

EXPLORING AFRO HAIR IS AN ENTRY TO
AFRO CULTURE

LET US WALK THIS JOURNEY WITH YOU!

JOIN LOVE & COILS TODAY

WWW.HAIRESSENTIALSCOMPANY.COM

SPECIAL THANKS TO MAX WEINBERG
FOR HELPING MAKING THIS GUIDE
POSSIBLE AND HIS DILIGENT WORK
ADVOCATING FOR ADOPTEES IN OUR
SCHOOL SYSTEM.

Made in the USA
Middletown, DE
30 August 2023

37393231R10035